A GATHER OF SHADOW

Mark Roper

DEDALUS PRESS

DUBLIN, IRELAND

ACKNOWLEDGEMENTS

Acknowledgements and thanks are due to the editors of the following, in which some of these poems, or versions of them, first appeared: *Abridged, An Cathach, Brass On Bronze, Did I Tell You?, Ink Bottle, Landing Places, Menu Poems, Molossus, New Hibernia Review, Not Only The Dark, Poems in Shop Windows, Poetry International Web, Poetry Ireland, Poetry Salzburg, Poets on Board, Shine On, Soul Feathers, Southword, Temenos, The Bow-Wow Shop, The Church Mouse, The Goose, The River Book, The Shop, The Stinging Fly* and *The Tablet*.

Some of the poems have been broadcast on RTE Radio 1's *Sunday Miscellany*.

Thanks to the staff at the Tyrone Guthrie Centre at Annaghmakerrig.

Very special thanks to James Harpur, Bill Tinley and Grace Wells for their careful reading and wise advice.

This book is dedicated to my sisters Ann and Sue.

COMHAIRLE CHONTAE ÁTHA CLIATH THEAS
SOUTH DUBLIN COUNTY LIBRARIES

COUNTY LIBRARY, TOWN CENTRE, TALLAGHT
TO RENEW ANY ITEM TEL: 462 0073
OR ONLINE AT www.southdublinlibraries.ie

Items should be returned on or before the last date below. Fines, as displayed in the Library, will be charged on overdue items.

First published in 2012 by
The Dedalus Press
13 Moyclare Road
Baldoyle
Dublin 13
Ireland

www.dedaluspress.com

ISBN 978 1 906614 59 1

Dedalus Press titles are represented in the UK by
Central Books, 99 Wallis Road, London E9 5LN
and in North America by Syracuse University Press, Inc.,
621 Skytop Road, Suite 110, Syracuse, New York 13244.

Cover image by the Dutch painter Felice,
www.atelier-felice.nl

The Dedalus Press receives financial assistance from
The Arts Council / An Chomhairle Ealaíon

CONTENTS

KEEP-NET

A GATHER OF SHADOW

KEEP-NET

River at Night

Its vegetable breath,
its mucky olive, soaked khaki coat.
Transparent hands
reaching out to finger fields,
pilfer the land's
few remaining pieces
of silver.
Out it stretches, where ash
and alder end,
a dull gleaming, neglected metal,
all there is to be seen.
Little winds flaming and lazing.
On a dead branch
an owl, a wicker of twigs
the slightest touch
could scatter. A shadow peels
off a shadow,
a night heron perhaps, perhaps
something else,
a shape too vague to translate.
All you can do now
is listen, to a train shunting
its slow tonnage,
to a snuffling creature trickling
spittle, a ghost soak
slurring its words, speaking its reek.

Falling

Swallow never stops – falls out of bed
at dawn and over the trees, fields, roads
and water, keeps falling all day long.
And if she stops on a wire it's only
to let it all catch up and then she's off
again, falling the whole day through,
as if she could find some edge or end
to things and fall clean out of day.
So, when I close my eyes to sleep, I start
to fall, through and out of all I know,
only to land with a bump suddenly back
in myself again, all there in one piece,
for where could there be to fall to
beyond the limit of skin, the limit of day?

The Forge

It seemed the world had forgotten the forge.
We didn't notice the smith, heaped on
a broken chair in shadow, until he spoke.
The great bellows he showed us lovingly,
the many different nails, the shoes, tongs, hammers
were buried under inches of dust,
sunken bullion on an ocean floor.
He moved like a man underwater,
breathing equipment disconnected.
He touched his face and the spot stayed white.

It seemed the world had forgotten the forge
but in through the door flew a hot coal,
a swallow, which from the darkness melted
the fresh metal, the sharp chink of her young.

Little Soul

after Hadrian's 'Animula'

Little soul,
curled inside like a cat,
turning up your nose
at the milk of everyday.

Little intimate,
exiled in flesh,
making the best
of the temporary.

When the senses shut,
when their door closes
behind you,
where will you go?

Little breath,
with no one
to take you in,
what will you be?

You who sneered
at appearances,
who said you saw
through things,

what will you do
without them?

Just

Just the grebe
on the lake
first thing.

Just the wedge
of its head
taking shape.

Then the swallow
out
of the boatshed.

Then the ink
of its wing
on the water.

Advent

Open the door
and there they are,
each with a gift
of itself

Darkness, Stillness, Silence

So patiently
they wait their turn,
forever at
the edge of things

Darkness, Stillness, Silence

Turn out the light,
invite them in,
bow your head, be
their anointed

Darkness, Stillness, Silence

Black Bull

Winter's doing its best
to wipe him out.
One minute an ice-house,
the next he's a riverbed.

Lost for days in mist,
razored raw by wind,
he's a black fact
frost doesn't credit.

Feet forgotten in mire
he has to stand for it,
hunched in his muscle,
no look in his eye.

The great roof of his neck
sags, starts to leak.
Through his skull's tunnel
the draughts pour.

Everyone's in but him
and all he can do
is let the worst occur
and let it occur again.

By spring he's gone
though there he is,
dancing down the fence
beside the cattle,

flicking up his dainty feet,
bellowing his raw joy,
thick strings of drool
dropping on fresh grass.

Thrush

Into the half-silence, the half-light,
the in-between leavings of winter,
thrush wallops a volley of song –
the stale air is nailed in amazement.

It's a blow-torch, a sandblast,
it's petrol poured into tired linings,
perished rubber, the dust and grease
coating the soul. And ignited.

And what more could you ask for
and who cares if the song's not for you?
You stumble out of sleep into
this sudden flood, raking flack –

this shocking dose of hope he'll repeat
dawn after dawn for days, flouting
the laws of privacy, cleansing
the webby lens. You at the foot

of his tree in your pyjamas, skin
riddled with his life-giving shot.

Keep-Net

O voice, this world
you'd catch and keep
shines and slips through
each word you shape.

This

Chanced on in trees by a road,
surely abandoned, an old terrier.

Ramming itself down burrows, rushing
from one dirty hole to another.

As if the only thing it knew to do
was hurt itself and hurt itself again.

We tried to keep our distance,
tried to shoo and shout it off.

It shrank back, circled, crept up.
Its hare lip, its filthy teeth.

Its shitty coat, the edge of menace
running through its running.

It shrank back, circled, crept up,
at last had me cornered

and lifted its head to bite, I thought –
but only looked. And looked.

And in that look, such longing.
Such open, unguarded need.

This world, which cares for nothing,
which teaches such lessons of loss,

which finds in the wounds of our eyes
such gratitude, such love for itself –

this world our only home.

Cardamoms

I've only to bite on a cardamom
to be back in my father's bedroom
in the hands of Iraqi soldiers,

Hussim and Lhani their names, perhaps –
I'm going by sound, no one now
to say how much of this is true –

who stayed with us three months,
who turned that room into a souk,
who sang softly behind their closed door,

who shyly took my shy mother to the shop
to choose and model dresses for their wives,
who threw us up in the air and caught us,

who kissed us with stinking moustaches,
who cooked on a small stove in that room,
first time we'd ever seen men cook,

who from time to time would conjure up
light white sticky cardamom cakes,
the like of which we'd never tasted before.

I've only to bite on a cardamom to see
their zigzag over the lawn in an old car
picked up for a song that neither could drive,

to see them hit the gatepost as they leave
and lurch out into traffic, into history.
I've only to break the shell, find the seed

on my tongue, chew the tough fibre down
to a bitter woody tangle I can neither swallow
nor spit out – that's all I have to remember.

Pheasant

Glimpsed from the car
cowering in a kerb
that emerald and cornelian mask,
its majesty hampered
by a snood of grimy snow.

One haughty eye
outstaring
its predicament.

The Garden

When you look round the garden
you see what it does look like,
what it was meant to look like,
what it will look like next year.

But, just before it disappears
at night, in the last of the light
you see the shape of each leaf
and the place of each leaf

become fixed, inevitable, right
beyond all accident and design.
You wouldn't change a thing.
And the more you see that

the more you long for morning,
for fork and spade and secateurs.

All Up

Water in the saltmarsh pools
trembling over footmarked mud
and hawthorn stooping under
sea-wind's thump and battery,
lapwing all lift-off and lapse
and freshening the race track
a shower of golden plover,
a shape-changing shimmer
the sky can't hold still;
chevrons of geese, creak
of their unoiled complaint,
the haunt-call of a curlew,
an oystercatcher's insistence,
a single wigeon whistling
to and from another world,
and even the stationary swans,
when a dog launches itself in
and doggypaddles towards them,
even the swans harness their carts,
haul the long improbable logs
of their bodies off the lake
and everything's up in the air
and all over the place save
for the cormorant caught
in monofilament, drowned,
and the moorhen in a channel
caught in monofilament, about
to drown and, by the time
we pass by again, drowned.

Robin Song

Spring

Out of balls of rust and dust
beaks emerge and open up
and in a trickle in a run
notes sprinkle pale sun

Autumn

Song slows down to mourning
for and from a blood-brown breast
as if an apple found a tongue
to grieve its own sweet flesh

Poulanassy

So much rain, the waterfall many times
normal size, heard half a mile away.
The placid pool at its feet in uproar,
water hurtling in circles, whipping froth
up into branches – haws hanging on, maroon,
wrinkled, each one sporting a raindrop.
Twigs in ancient lichen, ochre, silvergrey.

Through fields we followed a torrent,
bunching, jostling, lurching out of bounds.
Came to barbed wire, a pine plantation.
Once I'd have ploughed on: you, under protest,
would have too, we'd end up stuck, me pretending
we weren't, you thinking *Told you so*. Now
we turn and walk back together, the fall
pumping up the volume, spray from its grindstone
beginning to drench us, scent-sharpening,
sparkling on our skin in early dark.

Lough

Otters perhaps, the shadows
in low waves that crease
on occasion the lough:

their outlines supplied to go
with the fox on the path,
the yellow iris luminous still.

Sometimes like water
the texture of thought:
spilling into, giving

back to the world
what it seemed
for a moment to lack;

sometimes, closed as stone.
And the world not let
return the favour.

An otter not there
but there in a fold of water:
this brimming over

and then this being
in one's being, as an iris
is in an iris.

A GATHER OF SHADOW

Fields

At dusk I'm drawn to the back lane
to watch the new foal. It floats and folds
around its mother, a giddiness, an armful
of air barely touching the ground.

Over hedgerows the white flowers
whiten as darkness thickens.
Trees have settled to their long tasks,
easing new rings on their fingers.

Almost past the edge of hearing, making
their claim on the lateness, children call.
A sound like the memory of a sound.
A dog barks. A car comes and goes.

On the hill lights start to appear.
Swallows reel through the field.
Horse and foal have wandered away
and are lost in a gather of shadow.

Oar

You stood the oar they gave you
against the brick wall in the yard,
asking that when you touched
the smoothed, silvered wood
it might buoy you into air rung
by waterfowl, onto mirrored sky –
asking that it might bring back
those hours strung on soft splashes
which wired you in to the river
until the river rowed you,
rained into and sustained you,
a frill of water fraying off the blade
as you leant back and pulled,
leant back and pulled,
still able to work the world.

Sea Fret

The fret came down so thick and fast
you lost all sense of direction.
There was no one there to call to.

You swam round and round
until you thought you would drown.
At last the faintest whisper
of a wave led you back to shore.

You got dressed. Drove home.
Made breakfast. Told no one,
not a single word for twenty years.

You're back inside that fret again,
this time no shore can be found
and you're saying *I'm so sorry,*
I'm so sorry to let you all down.

In Between

You are down at the brink
under the black poplars,
ready to give up the ghost.

Each time the boatman comes
he finds no coin in your mouth
and will not take you.

We can hear your *tut*,
impatient *tut*. We know
soon you will decide

to creep away, nip under a fence
and swim across yourself.
Neither life nor death

will know where to find you –
you'll be swimming somewhere
in between and in the dark

you won't be able to tell
which shore is which
and you would never ask.

The Far Shore

We took you down to visit your friend Dora,
still living by the sea the two of you
once swam in daily, come rain or shine.

She was a long time coming to the door.
When she did, she greeted you warmly,
then turned to us and said *But I thought
you were going to bring your mother along.*

Silence

In your room you sit
with Silence.

Just a few small things
beside you.

She's asked you to clear
some space for her.

She doesn't leave now
when we come in.

When we talk
she tries to interrupt.

You keep looking
across at her.

We can almost
see her too.

We too begin to fall
under her spell.

Soon she insists
we leave.

She wants you
all to herself.

Wildflowers

You taught me most of what I know of flowers –
their names of course, their habitats, their scents.
And somehow, subtly, not by word of mouth
and much more than knowledge, a love for them.

Now the names of even the most common
escape you. And though I try to teach you
what you once taught me, you don't really care.
Where you're going, names make no difference.

I'll not persist with them. Nor will I pick
what flowers I find to bring: I know
they'll not survive. Instead I'll hold my hands
around a bunch of living, growing stems.

All that matters, their shy independence –
that this might be held, by being let go.

Lough Mora

When it was clear you'd not last
much longer, I took you with me
to try to find Lough Mora.

Not where it should have been.
Forestry tracks turned and tangled
round themselves, until we had
to make a guess that we'd find it
behind that ridge, under Knockanaffrin.

We left the track, worked our way
over cut stumps, rocks, holes,
tussocks, rushes, bog, streams;
fought through stunted firs;
shared that good feeling of not
knowing where we were going.

Over the ridge, there it was,
small, a neatly folded blanket
at the mountain's foot, guarded
by two giant boulders covered
in moss and the soft ears
of Saint Patrick's Cabbage.

The water, peat-stained, clear,
hung still as silence over its bed
of rounded, overlapping stones.
You stripped, waded straight in
and began to swim away.

Can I come with you?
Not this time, no.

Last Breath

Though you couldn't swallow,
had taken no food for weeks,
your breathing wouldn't stop.

In and out, slow and steady
as the stroke of an oar,
it just kept on going.

As if that breathing
had become a pair of oars,
rowing of their own accord.

Each stroke rowing you
further away from us,
deeper into the distance

until, with the slightest click,
those oars were docked.

That Day

I walked up the beach
after swimming,
saltwater like flame
on my skin, my feet
printing the stones.

In a rockpool slicks
and slivers of light.
Moist wader voicings.
Each pebble shining,
each and every one.

Cold

In that white room,
your cold form.

Not stone-cold,
colder than stone,

a cold so intense
it had to be living.

As if, when we lifted
the veil, such cold

could burn colour
back into you, allow

your hands to relax
and receive the sprigs

of rosemary, beech
and winter jasmine

we place on them.

Last Look

As soon as we opened the door –
Ann and I had slipped back
for a last look – we could hear you:
O do get on with it, for pity's sake!

Public

After they had removed your body
and after Ann had tidied the house,
one room was still full of metal and rubber,
all the scaffolding needed to keep you up,
cushions, hoist, frames, wheelchair,
bath-lift, special bed, alarm.
Props waiting for another stage.

It had been such a show. So public.
And you were such a private soul.
You who hated the show of any feeling.
As soon as they began to treat you,
as soon as you were touched, you withdrew.
You'd never have said, but it's there in photos,
that set of mouth, that puzzle in your eyes.

Like a bird whose broken wing heals
in captivity, but which won't even try
to fly again, you lost the will to live.
All that weakness on show, you grew
more and more helpless. Unbearable,
never to be really on your own.

Unable to find a quiet corner to die,
you hid, in the only place you could,
inside yourself. You left your face behind,
crawled away deeper and deeper.
It took you a long time to manage.
But you got there in the end.

Rose

November rose,
last of the last, framed
in the breaking of days.

Having come so far,
with nothing to go on,
nowhere to go.

More-than-ever rose,
up to your eyes
in the rooks' cold court.

Rose on a river of darkness.

The Last Place

At the end of the short ceremony
none of us could keep our eyes from
the undertaker's attempt to settle
the small stone. The square he'd cut out
wasn't quite big enough. He tried
to widen it with his heel, he took
his short spade and tried again,
he fetched a black plastic bag,
laid it over the stone, trod down
with the toe of a polished black shoe.

Earlier we had taken the bag
to the beach, swam with it, shaken
a handful of ash each into the sea.
I remembered how as children
we'd swum in a wide bay somewhere
and your one false tooth had fallen out,
how we had tried to mark the spot
and how that night we came back
when the tide had ebbed and found it
on the uncovered, puckered sand.

How you picked it up, put it back.
How your smile was restored.

Distance

Though you can see for miles
across the lake to the mountain,
and though you can imagine
all that lies beyond, ridge
after ridge and the rivers
joining to make their slow,
swollen fall to the sea;
though you think you can say
how far the sunlight travels
to wash the ears of ivy
and make the hawkweed blaze,
to warm the stone's cold shoulder
and the wary heart;
though you think as you swim
how you used to swim with her,
how you'd lie on your backs
and press your feet together
and race each other back to shore;
though you've reached, you think,
some idea of distances involved,
how things are so far apart
yet one and the same –
it will be, you will find,
as nothing to the distance
opened by the loon's cry
that first night; and, in the wake
of that cry, the silence.

Shell

On a beach
you might find
a scrap of shell

so small you will
wonder why
you noticed it,

so clean you will
not be able
to say what life

it might once
have housed,
so thoroughly

has all trace
of that life
been consumed.

In the warmth
of your palm
it seems

to give off
a faint,
familiar light.

When you put it
down with all
the others,

all the others,
when you walk
away, it will not

be held, not
be warmed, not
be found again.

Michaelmas

Daisies a late purple.
Dahlias all rouge and wreck.
A good time to go.

Tremble-nets of midges,
silver veins of contrail
in ash-blue evening sky.

A cloak of broken rose,
red admirals rising
in a soundless swarm.

All things on the verge.
Quickness of this world
its quietness again.

Leaves

It was such a long autumn, dry and bright.
The leaves hung on, November, December.

When they finally began to fall, they made
deep drifts against the front door, blowing

inside when that door was opened, getting
everywhere, under chairs, into slippers.

Even now I'm finding them outside, packets
hidden under Spring growth, last letters.

Treecreeper

Up the broad trunk of a eucalyptus
a treecreeper creeps, so well camouflaged
it can hardly be seen – though its beak,
a curved needle, can be imagined,
working so furiously at the bark
it might well be stitching to that bark
the edge of a sheet behind which
it could make itself even less visible.

Reaching the top, the bird lets itself fall,
leafbrown, charcoal, a tiny burning book.
There were feelings, but they were not to be
spoken of. Once only you broke that rule:
you told me you wished you were dead.
To that wish you never referred again.

Damn

Family holidays started at three a.m.,
loaded in blankets into the black Minx,
sleeping through empty London, heading west.
Detours to have a picnic, stretch our legs.
Meeting a coach in high-hedged, narrow lanes.
The last few miles. Arrival. Exploration.
All taken care of. All done for us children.

One summer it rained the whole time.
Cooped up we fought and squabbled constantly.
Near the end you dropped a glass jug.
The word *Damn* broke from your lips, first time
we'd ever heard you swear. It left us speechless.
All that pent up force. All that loss of face.
The word filled the room, had to be ignored –

as if the jug, smashed, had at once re-formed,
continued to serve, dared us to notice.

Crossing

Swallows queuing up
to take on water,
skimming the surface
of a pond to fill
their small tanks.

Soon they'll be gone,
away across the seas
to their second home.
I'll keep eyes peeled
for their return.

April, I might be
on the phone perhaps
when the first one
makes its way past
the narrow window.

I might be sitting
where I'd ring you
to say hello, and hello,
and hello: a phone
held to your ear.

You might have heard;
wouldn't have answered.
Silence your wing,
your means of crossing.
Your brave last word.

Pollen

One lily
from the wreath
I kept,

for months now
stood in a vase
on my desk,

the petals brown,
stiffened twists
of tissue,

one stem bent
and bare, anthers
still hanging, ,

each tip still
muzzled in pollen:
just a grain

falling now
and then
beside your photo.

19.9.08

Today would have been
your ninetieth birthday.

I lie in bed and listen
to wood pigeons,

their *rou-cou-cou*
drifting through trees.

I count ninety rounds
to keep in mind,

to cover my head today –
like the headscarf

you'd tie under your chin,
or your wedding veil

blown above your head
as you wait in a photograph

to enter the church.
But I keep losing count.

Or when I get to ninety
the pigeons keep going

and their calls decline
to add up to anything.

Treading Water

It'll be in the last place you look
you'd say when I'd lost something.

And if you were looking for scissors
you'd make two fingers scissorblades.

And if I had a spot you'd prick it
with a needle red from match-flame.

And *I'll crown you* you'd say when cross
with me *I'll crown you one of these days.*

And after you'd taught me to swim
you showed me how to tread water.

Just wiggle your legs and arms a bit,
you'd say. *Trust the water to hold you.*

Summer Snowflakes

A swan can break your arm.
I could believe that today,
watching one skid across the river
to scare off another pair,
around a stretched blade of neck
its wings stiff as a hilt.

I remember how one day
you vanished under a river
when a swan flew straight at you,
and I wish you could resurface
here, climb into the canoe
and come with us up the Clodiagh
to see the summer snowflakes.

All white bonnet and slender neck
they're gooseherds, tending
unruly gaggles of marigolds.
You'd call them Loddon Lilies,
you'd wonder with us how
they came to be here, whether
they'd escaped from a garden.

Their bonnets slip off and on,
off and on, their necks break
and heal in water where I see
you still, will always see you.
How fresh the river's breath
when we return to the Suir,
and how innocent it seems,
that empty, gleaming reach.